GW00361022

Welcome to **'How2Become: The insider's guide to becoming a Police Communications Officer'**. This guide has been designed to help you prepare for, and pass the tough selection process for joining the police as a 999 call handler.

The selection process to join the police is highly competitive. Approximately 65,000 people apply to join the police every year in a variety of different roles. But what is even more staggering is that only approximately 7,000 of those applicants will be successful. You could view this as a worrying statistic, or alternatively you could view it that you are determined to be one of the 7,000 who are successful. Armed with this insider's guide, you have certainly taken the first step to passing the Police Communications Officer selection process.

The guide itself has been split up into useful sections to make it easier for you to prepare for each stage. Read each section carefully and take notes as you progress. Don't ever give up on your dreams; if you really want to become a police communications officer then you can do it. The way to approach the selection process is to embark on a programme of 'in depth' preparation, and this guide will show you exactly how to do that.

The selection process is not easy to pass. Unless that is, you put in plenty of preparation. Your preparation must be focused in the right areas, and also be comprehensive enough to give you every chance of success. This guide will teach you how to be a successful candidate.

The way to pass the selection process is to develop your own skills and experiences around the qualities and competencies that are required to become a communications officer. Many candidates who apply to join the police will be unaware that the competencies even exist. As you progress through this guide you will find that these important elements of the role will form the foundations of your preparation. So, the first step in your preparation, and before we go any further, is to get hold of a copy of the qualities and competencies required for this role. They will usually form part of your application pack but if they don't, you can obtain a copy of them by visiting the website of the force you are applying to join.

If you need any further help with any elements of the selection process, including tests and interview, then we offer a wide range of products to assist you. These are all available through our online shop www.how2become.com. We also run a 1-day intensive 999 Call Handlers Course. Details are available at the website **www.999CallHandler.co.uk**.

Once again, thank you for your custom and we wish you every success in your pursuit to becoming a police communications officer.

Work hard, stay focused and be what you want…

Best wishes,

The how2become team

The How2become Team

P.S. Attend a 1-Day police communications officer training course run by former police officers!

Go to **www.999CallHandler.co.uk** to find out more.

CONTENTS

CHAPTER 1 INTRODUCTION 1

WHY WORK WITHIN THE POLICE FORCE? 2

WHAT IS A POLICE COMMUNICATIONS OFFICER? 4

HOW DO YOU BECOME A POLICE COMMUNICATIONS OFFICER? 6

CHAPTER 2 WHAT DOES IT TAKE TO BECOME A POLICE COMMUNICATIONS OFFICER 7

ESSENTIAL SKILLS AND COMPETENCIES FOR A POLICE COMMUNICATIONS OFFICER 7

EXAMPLE JOB DESCRIPTION 9

EXAMPLE PERSON SPECIFICATION 13

BENEFITS ASSOCIATED WITH THE ROLE OF POLICE COMMUNICATIONS OFFICER 15

ASSESSING YOUR SUITABILITY FOR THE JOB 16

ASK YOURSELF SOME SERIOUS QUESTIONS 17

HOW TO GET THE SKILLS AND COMPETENCIES YOU NEED 20

IS THE POLICE COMMUNICATIONS OFFICER JOB RIGHT FOR YOU? 26

CHAPTER 3 THE APPLICATION AND SELECTION PROCESS 27

WHERE ARE VACANCIES ADVERTISED? 27

OUTLINE OF THE SELECTION PROCESS 28

ON THE JOB TRAINING 29

ELIGIBILITY FOR EMPLOYMENT AS A POLICE COMMUNICATIONS OFFICER – VETTING 30

A NOTE ON CRIMINAL CONVICTIONS 32

CHAPTER 4 APPLYING FOR A POLICE COMMUNICATIONS OFFICER ROLE 35

HOW TO APPLY FOR A POLICE COMMUNICATIONS OFFICER ROLE 35

HOW TO COMPLETE THE APPLICATION FORM 36

THE PURPOSE OF THE APPLICATION FORM 37

OVERVIEW OF THE SELECTION PROCESS 38

HOW TO COMPLETE THE APPLICATION FORM 40

GUIDELINES ON COMPLETING THE APPLICATION FORM – SECTION BY SECTION COMMENTARY 46

SAMPLE RESPONSES TO PERSON SPECIFICATION CRITERIA 51

TEN TOP TIPS AND ONE USEFUL ACRONYM FOR COMPLETING THE APPLICATION FORM 61

CHAPTER 5 THE ASSESSMENT CENTRE 65

WHAT IS THE PURPOSE OF THE ASSESSMENT CENTRE? 66

TESTING AT THE ASSESSMENT CENTRE 67

HOW TO PREPARE FOR THE ASSESSMENT CENTRE 69

IF YOU ARE TAKING LITERACY AND NUMERACY TESTS 70

A NOTE ON ROLE PLAY 72

FOUR TIPS FOR HANDLING ROLE PLAY 73

PRACTICE TESTS 75

CREATING A POSITIVE IMPRESSION 75

SEVEN TOP TIPS WHEN ATTENDING AN ASSESSMENT CENTRE 76

TIPS FOR PSYCHOMETRIC TESTS 77

CHAPTER 6 THE INTERVIEW 83

SAMPLE INTERVIEW QUESTIONS AND RESPONSES 85

CONCLUSION 105

APPENDIX A POLICE COMMUNICATIONS OFFICER SAMPLE APPLICATION FORM 107

how2become

CHAPTER ONE

INTRODUCTION

According to various statistics, at any one time, one in five of us would like to change our job if we possibly could. In today's world, job satisfaction is not simply about taking a pay cheque at the end of each month. Today's jobseekers are looking for something more; they are seeking that intangible element that brings fulfilment and a sense of purpose to their lives.

According to the National Careers Service, there are four essential elements that people look for in a rewarding career:

- A job that reflects who we really are.
- Something that allows us to play to our strengths.
- A role that enables us to contribute positively to our local communities and society as a whole.
- The ability to 'give something back'.

All of those aspirations are certainly worthy, but is it really possible to have all of that within your career? We'll come back to that in a moment. Firstly, let's consider the facts; most of us in employment spend five days a week in our working environment. Over the course of a typical career, that equates to one third of our lives. That is an eye-opening statistic by anyone's standards isn't it?

So, coming back to our question above is it possible to change your career or your current role to find something that meets all of our aspirations?

We believe so, yes, but to achieve this you will need to take relevant career advice, understand your skills and strengths and thoroughly research the careers that you feel have the potential to meet the above criteria for you personally.

Here, we will consider one position that has the potential to meet all of the elements required for a rewarding career as defined above by the National Careers Service. We will also provide you with the information you need to make an informed decision about whether or not this role meets with your own personal career aspirations.

That position is the role of **Police Communications Officer**, sometimes referred to as a 999 Call Handler.

WHY WORK WITHIN THE POLICE FORCE?

The Police Force in England and Wales employs over 130,000[1] staff across the UK and is one of the country's largest employers. When we think of police officers, we typically think of the front line roles, the so-called 'bobbies on the beat' dramatically portrayed on our television screens

---

[1] Figures provided by *The Guardian* 2012.

in series such as 'The Bill'.

Front line police work isn't necessarily for everyone, however, but there are many more opportunities open to potential candidates considering a career in the police force that would thrive in such an environment, yet are deterred by the aspects of the nature of front line work. These posts include administrative roles, finance, human resources, call handling positions, data analysts and even librarians.

Positions within the police force are often seen as tough and unpredictable but they can be very rewarding. The role of the Police Communications Officer is no different. You will be the type of person who relishes a challenge and is willing to work hard to adapt and learn the necessary skills for this essential role.

One thing you can be sure of with this position, however, is the ability to give something back to your local community.

As a Police Communications Officer you have the opportunity to make a significant contribution towards improving the safety of the local community. You will be helping to make the world a safer place for your family, friends, neighbours and your local community in this vital role.

Perhaps you know colleagues or friends who have been burgled or mugged? Perhaps you have even been the victim of a burglary or violence yourself. If you called the emergency services you would no doubt have been put through to a 999 Call Handler. Do you remember how they responded to your distress? Were they helpful, patient and reassuring? That could be you!

If you are seeking a worthwhile role that contributes positively to your local community and society as a whole, then this certainly fits the bill.

In terms of your own career development and making an informed decision on whether it is a position that you will actually enjoy, make sure you consider the following:

- Every day is completely different to the last – literally two situations many never be exactly the same!
- Ample opportunities for career advancement are available for ambitious applicants.
- You will continually be presented with challenges as well as the opportunity to learn and grow within your working environment.
- You will be making a difference to your community and to the public at large.

Let's look at it in a little more detail.

WHAT IS A POLICE COMMUNICATIONS OFFICER?

A Police Communications Officer is the first point of contact for all 999 emergency and high priority calls for police assistance. It is estimated that around 80,000 emergency calls are made within the UK every single day. The role of Communications Officer is a wide and varied position comprising early, late and night shifts. It is a twenty-four hour a day, seven days a week role, throughout the year.

999 Call Handlers are required to handle large volumes of telephone calls, obtain and record accurate information, assess the situation and level of police response required and initiate the appropriate police action as rapidly as possible. Often they may be required to handle several emergency situations simultaneously, all of it taking place within the confines of an intensely pressured environment. Every time

you respond to a telephone call, it's impossible to predict what type of call you will be responding to.

A Police Communications Officer is the lynchpin in communication between the police force and the general public. It is a highly demanding, highly stressful position yet can also be extremely rewarding. As a Police Communications Officer you will deal with calls from the tedious to the deadly serious on a daily basis. It is certainly not your standard nine to five job, nor is it for the fainthearted. From people being mugged to someone complaining about their neighbour's dog, no two days will ever be the same.

In order to carry out this role successfully, you will be required to demonstrate key skills and competencies to enable you to handle high volumes of distressed callers in a calm, professional but firm manner. The diverse range of skills required will be discussed in more detail in Chapter 2.

To put the significance of the role within context, the Metropolitan Police Force alone covers an area of 620 square miles and a population of 7.2 million. On a typical day, Police Communications Officers working for the Metropolitan Police can be expected to handle around 6,000 emergency calls alone. The number of non-emergency calls can also reach 15,000 every day.

That is every day of the year!

That's not the end of the story of course. The level of emergency calls increases dramatically during summer and can reach peaks of around 10,000 calls every day. Equally, Thames Valley Police receives 6,500 emergency (999) calls and 21,000 non-emergency calls (101) every week.

If we haven't completely deterred you, then read on!

HOW DO YOU BECOME A POLICE COMMUNICATIONS OFFICER?

In this book we will examine in detail the complete recruitment and selection process, from start to finish. We will study a sample job description for this role, a person specification detailing the experience, skills and competencies needed and how to gain these skills if you don't have them already. The chances are you probably possess a number of key skills, although you may not be aware of them yet. As part of the selection process for becoming a Police Communications Officer, candidates are required to undergo a series of rigorous assessments. This includes completing a competency based application form, attending an Assessment Centre, participating in a competency based interview and a series of practical and psychometric tests.

We will also provide detailed information on the type of responses you should include in your application form, consider the variety of interview questions you may face and provide information on how to handle the Assessment Centre. We will even provide access to on-line audio testing to help to build your confidence in dealing with example scenarios, which may be typical of the type of testing you will experience at the Assessment Centre.

So, if you are serious about your career as a Police Communications Officer, then let's start by looking at the role itself and what it actually entails.

CHAPTER TWO

WHAT DOES IT TAKE TO BECOME A POLICE COMMUNICATIONS OFFICER?

A Police Communications Officer is a demanding yet rewarding role which requires a unique blend of skills. To give you an idea of the formal requirements for the role, we've included a typical sample job description for the position below, together with a person specification. But first, let's look at the essential skills and competencies for the role.

ESSENTIAL SKILLS AND COMPETENCIES FOR A POLICE COMMUNICATIONS OFFICER

To consider this position seriously, you will need to possess a number of core competencies, including the following:

- A good level of education which demonstrates competent literacy skills and an ability to think logically. Normally 5 GCSE's at Grade 'C' or above are recommended although not all **police forces specify that number**. At the very least, candidates should possess 4, including English and Maths.
- Experience of a customer facing environment; the post holder should have extensive experience of regular interaction with individuals of all ages. It will be advantageous if this has been gained within a call centre environment but it isn't essential to be successful in your application. The key is your ability to clearly demonstrate that you possess the necessary skills.
- Experience of working within a computerised environment is preferred, coupled with an ability to understand and operate IT systems. A working knowledge of Microsoft Office is also useful. Proficient keyboard skills and an ability to type from audio at a speed of around 30/35 wpm is also required.
- You will need to demonstrate an ability to pose relevant questions coupled with listening skills.
- Strong communication skills, both verbally and written are vital to this role.

Candidates lacking aspects of the above experience will not necessarily be rejected.

The ability to demonstrate that you possess the ability to learn these skills will prove significant in the application process.

EXAMPLE JOB DESCRIPTION

A typical job description for a Police Communications Officer is as follows:

Reports to: Sergeant or Supervisor

Responsible for: This position is not responsible for any staff.

Police Communications Officer: Main Purpose of the Position

- To provide a complete communication and support service to both the public and operational officers while ensuring a customer focused approach at all times particularly when dealing with distressed members of the public.
- To answer all calls for the service received in the Force Control Room. Each incident reported must be risk assessed and graded in accordance with the individual Force policy. Appropriate action must be initiated.
- To record crimes and missing persons reported by both officers and members of the public.

Principal Duties:

- Answer both emergency and non-emergency calls and establish the nature and risk of reported incidents in a calm and professional manner. These calls vary in nature from distressed members of the public to hoax calls.

In addition, there may be calls referred internally and a number of regular or routine calls.

- Listen carefully to the call while quickly and accurately recording what is being said. All calls must be recorded using the relevant equipment ensuring that all necessary information is obtained correctly and completely to enable proper evaluation of the incident and circumstances.
- Evaluate the nature of calls and ensure that appropriate action is undertaken, including redeploying adequate and suitable police attendance, in accordance with individual Force Policy and Home Office Guidelines to effectively deal with the problem.
- Transmit and receive radio messages on various channels using computerised equipment, prioritising each message as appropriate.
- Identify and report immediately to the relevant commander incidents that are, or have the potential to develop into, high risk matters often in highly pressurised situations.
- Receive and record reports of crime and missing persons accurately on to Force systems in line with current Force standards, Crime Recording Standards and Home Office Rules.

- Where possible, resolve non-emergency incidents through providing advice to callers by utilising the appropriate policies and legal procedures.
- Carry out relevant checks using the Police National Computer (PNC) and create records, as required, following set procedures in strict accordance with the Data Protection Act.
- Carry out enquiries with Force intelligence systems in connection with the management of incidents and place results where appropriate on the incident. In addition, the post holder is required to carry out such checks at the request of operational officers.
- Maintain and examine various records as required. This may include information on a range of issues covering local matters and information on solicitors on call, medical staff, interpreters and so on.
- Provide support to other Control Room Operatives (for example, Dispatch). This will include 'call backs', intelligence checks and log keeping.
- Allocate scheduled appointments to members of the public.
- Complete any other reasonable task in support of Force Control Room business.

Of course, a job description may detail the technical requirements of carrying out the role successfully, but what personal skills will you need to make it in the role?

On paper it may sound exciting but the reality of working in a highly pressured position is very different. Police Communications Officers quite literally deal with life and death situations so an ability to remain calm under pressure is a pre-requisite, as is the ability to maintain an emotional detachment from the situation. You cannot, under any circumstances, allow your own personal life to influence your work. All external influences must be put to the back of your mind from the moment you walk through the door to your desk.

For example, Police Communications Officers are often required to keep a caller on the line until police officers arrive at the scene which requires a unique skill set. Do you possess those skills?

Let's look more closely at the Person Specification for the role.

EXAMPLE PERSON SPECIFICATION

The personal skills you will need to demonstrate for the Police Communications Officer role are as follows:

- Demonstrate outstanding communication skills, both written and verbal. Candidates must possess the ability to quickly establish both the customer needs and the nature of the policing response required.
- Commitment to providing a consistently high level of customer service
- Demonstrate excellent ability to listen and subsequently interpret information before conducting an accurate risk assessment based on the information provided.
- Show resilience in pressured situations, especially when dealing with stressful situations and often extremely emotional customers.
- Ability to make decisions quickly and appropriately based on the information provided.
- Demonstrate an ability to work effectively within a team and a willingness to support their colleagues in achieving their goals.
- Show an adaptability to both learn and retain relevant information.

- Display an appropriate level of assertiveness when necessary.
- Display skills in basic research and extracting information when relevant to customer needs.
- Show a clear focus on and understanding of community needs.
- Demonstrate a clearly high level of self-motivation and an ability to work with minimal supervision. This should be evidenced through high levels of productivity.
- Demonstrate a positive and flexible attitude and an ability to adapt to changing situations and new working practices.
- Display an appropriate degree of awareness pertaining to equality and diversity issues where relevant to this position.
- Demonstrate the ability to multi-task in undertaking administration duties while prioritising the answering of 999 calls.
- Work to a consistently high and effective standard.
- Quick and accurate typing and IT literacy skills, for example, Microsoft Office, coupled with the ability to record information accurately and quickly. The ability to listen, interpret relevant information and type while speaking with callers is essential.

- The willingness and ability to work in a flexible 24/7 environment, all year round, is essential to this position.

The ability to speak a second language is also advantageous.

BENEFITS ASSOCIATED WITH THE ROLE OF POLICE COMMUNICATIONS OFFICER

A career within the Police Force offers a number of attractive benefits including:

Salary: Police employees across all police forces are normally paid a competitive salary commensurate with their role which is agreed prior to commencement of employment. To give you an idea, the current quoted figures for the Metropolitan Police show a basic salary of £20,984, together with an additional 10% flexibility allowance and a 20% shift allowance upon completion of training. Annual increments are achievable on the basic pay up to £24,015[2].

A London Location Allowance is also payable as applicable which will depend on the specific location but can range from £1,800 per annum to £3,466.

Each police force will vary and again, we stress that the above example incorporates the London 'weighting allowance' common to many positions based in the capital.

---

[2] Figures correct as of January 2013

Working Hours: Hours are normally 37 hours per week for full-time staff and will require flexible shift working on a 24/7 basis all year round. Shift allowances are also paid to shift workers.

Annual Leave Entitlement: Holiday entitlement varies but normally starts at around 25 days per year plus standard statutory days and calculated on a pro-rata basis for any part-time employees.

Pensions: All police employees are entitled to join their local government pension scheme or the state earnings related pension scheme (SERPS). There is also the option to take out a private pension.

Sick Leave: Policies with regard to sick leave may vary depending on the individual police force. Employee entitlements to payments for sick leave increase the longer the period of continuous service.

ASSESSING YOUR SUITABILITY FOR THE JOB

While it may sound like a fascinating 'never a dull moment' type of role, the successful candidate must exude a subtle confidence and assertiveness. You will be dealing with a diverse range of situations, ranging from the innocuous – such as the proverbial 'cat in a tree' scenario – to life threatening. You must therefore possess a degree of emotional intelligence and maturity, together with a level of self-awareness.

ASK YOURSELF SOME SERIOUS QUESTIONS:

How do you view your job, is it simply a way of paying the bills or do you enjoy work?

A Police Communications Officer's role is not simply a 'job'. You cannot afford to have an off or a slack day. If that is your view of work, perhaps it isn't for you. As we have mentioned previously, your own personal issues cannot interfere with your working life in this role.

Think about your current role and consider what transferable skills you may have in your background. The following questions may help you to evaluate your suitability for the role:

- ***Have you worked in a call centre environment before?*** If so, how did you handle issues such as customer complaints? Think back to the worst customer complaint or call that you handled, and then multiply the effect of that on you personally by at least ten for the situations you will face as a Police Communications Officer.
- ***Can you think 'on your feet'?*** Are you able to think quickly and logically, can you make logical evaluations of urgent situations? If you tend to fall automatically into panic mode and run around like the proverbial headless chicken then you may need to think again with this role.
- ***What transferable skills do you possess within your CV?*** By transferable skills we mean, for example, outstanding communication skills, an ability to organise and delegate coupled with an ability to remain composed under extremely pressured conditions. In summary, transferable skills are those you have acquired and developed within another role that can be

used in a Police Communications role with the same level of competency.

- ***Are you given a degree of autonomy to allow you to handle situations?*** Can you cope when left to make vital decisions alone? On occasion, the role of Police Communications Officer requires you to do just that. Previous experience of handling sensitive situations on your own may prove to be an advantage in your application.
- ***Can you multi-task?*** Can you type quickly and record information as people are speaking to you – and possibly deal with distractions in the background too? A Communications Officer's role requires you to remain focused at all times.
- ***What are your top five achievements within your CV or during your career?*** Do they demonstrate any of the skills within the person specification detailed above? Can you provide examples of where you have managed several situations under extreme pressure simultaneously?
- ***If this is your first job, where in your college or university life can you demonstrate the skills for this job?*** Have you handled conflict within a team or association you were a member of? Have you managed heated debates?
- ***Do you have natural empathy and compassion with people?*** Where and when? You will need to be able to provide specific examples of this.
- ***What is the most stressful situation you have encountered in your life, whether personally, at work or both?*** – and we do mean stressful, not simply a

wardrobe malfunction prior to a night out. The definition of stressful will mean completely different things to different people. What does 'stress' mean to you?

- ***What are your long-term career goals?*** As we've mentioned previously, this isn't simply a job, it requires anti-social hours and you will literally be dealing with life and death situations. Not all of these situations will end happily. How resilient are you? You may read reports in the newspapers about multiple vehicle pile-ups on the roads which result in fatalities and consider them to be sad and shocking. The difference is that in this role you may well find yourself at the centre of a situation where you are required to co-ordinate responses to one of these accidents.
- ***Have you worked shifts before?*** If not, try and imagine how you would feel working all night and getting home at 7am in the morning for example. Your life at times will become out of sync with those around you who may be working standard days.
- ***What are the reasons for applying for this position?*** If it is all about the money you can earn, that is the wrong reason to be applying. As we have previously stated, this is not a role for the fainthearted!
- ***Can you separate your own challenges in your daily life from your professional life?*** This is one job where your ability to do just that may mean the difference between success and failure in your application.
- ***How will the role of Communications Officer impact your family and social life?*** You may not be working certain shifts on set days, the pattern may vary so it will greatly affect your daily life and sleep patterns. If you

are someone who functions at their peak when working regular days and hours, or if you struggle with working a night shift, you will seriously need to reconsider the role of Communications Officer. On top of that you will need to consider the actual day to day responsibilities of the position too.

All of these questions require careful and reasoned consideration. We encourage you not to simply shrug your shoulders and think that you will 'cope' when the situation arises. These are all serious considerations to enable you to understand your motivation behind applying for this role.

Police Communications Officers come from a variety of backgrounds and ultimately it is your ability to meet the criteria in the person specification which will be relevant to your application. Experience within a busy call handling centre will be an advantage coupled with the ability to handle emergency situations with a calm and reasoning mind.

HOW TO GET THE SKILLS AND COMPETENCIES YOU NEED

If you scrutinise your background and career history to date, you may well find that you have some if not many of the skills and competencies required.

Key Skills and Competencies

Let's reconsider the key skills and competencies that you need for this job.

They are:

- Effective communication skills
- Customer service skills

- Listening skills
- Problem solving
- Confidence and assertiveness
- Ability to adapt quickly
- Self-motivated
- Focused.

If we look at the CVs or covering letters of most applicants in a random selection of jobs, you will see most of these skills are claimed by most applicants within the first few lines.

EXERCISE

We suggest a short exercise here to focus your mind on your own personal skills and competencies. This will also assist when it comes to the application process. Take each one of the skills we extracted above from the key competencies for the position of Police Communications Officer. Write them down on the left hand side of a sheet of paper and leave plenty of space. Once you have done that, take a look at your CV and in particular, what you consider to be your top five achievements.

Do any of those achievements require any of the skills we've highlighted? Think about what was required for you on a day-to-day basis. Most positions require good communication skills and a degree of self motivation.

If you don't feel that your achievements sufficiently demonstrate those key skills, can you think of specific examples of situations during your working life when you displayed any of the competencies listed above?

Against each one you might also want to mark them down on a level of 1 to 10 as to how much of each trait or skill you needed to use in that particular job. This will enable you to get an idea of your particular strengths and weaknesses.

We've included an example of how it might look to give you the general idea:

Skills & Competencies	Example From Top 5 Achievements/General Experience	How much skill was required? 1 (low) to 10 (high)
Communication	Team Leader Role – Through communicating a new sales strategy with my team we exceeded our quarterly sales target by 15% for three consecutive quarters. Communication and co-ordination with other departments was essential to achieve this.	7
Customer service	Assistant Retail Manager – This was a daily customer facing role requiring regular interaction with the public. Under my supervision, we were rated 9.5 out of 10 when we were 'Mystery Shopped' and all of our staff won a weekend away.	5

Listening	Telesales Position – Resolved an issue with a client who enquired about a particular brand of computer. We concluded together that a laptop would be a more suitable purchase for her. We discussed her needs and various brands and she was able to buy one well within her budget with my guidance.	8
Problem solving	Recruitment Consultant – For one client booking we lacked sufficient staffing numbers for a hospitality event. I assessed availability and offered an alternative to the client which still meant that their needs were still met and the event was a success.	8
Confidence and Assertiveness	Telemarketing Team Leader – When our weekly figures were down as we were fulfilling orders my boss gave us an 'informal' warning. I confidently defended our role, knowing the sales totals and he ultimately apologised. We later received a commendation!	7

Ability to adapt quickly	Office Manager Role – Successfully sourced a product for a customer when the sales department was unavailable due to a conference, despite it not being within my remit.	7
Self motivated	Call Centre Position – Regularly achieved higher targets on my KPIs (key performance indicators). Our manager set agreed call rates but we were expected to 'get on with it'.	9
Focused	HR Assistant Role – Developed new procedures that complied with change in employment laws reflecting attention to detail	6

You may find during this exercise that you have identified certain gaps within your current skill set which isn't unusual, particularly if you are in the early stages of your career or you have recently completed your education and are seeking your first full-time position. If that's the case, there are steps you can take to improve your skills in those areas.

Let's take customer service as an example. If you do not work in a customer facing role now, it is worth considering the following points:

- Did you ever subsidise any college work with part-time jobs that required dealing with the public?
- Alternatively, can you request additional training from your line manager in your current job?
- Always remember that 'customer service' can apply to working with colleagues from other departments. Marketing departments often liaise with sales departments to provide services to them – that is a form of 'customer service'.

Suggestions

If your company has placed a hold on further training at this time, there may be local evening classes that you can attend. Many training companies also offer free places for first time attendees on seminars which focus on a variety of work related training topics, such as improving communication skills, problem solving and customer service among others.

Typing Skills

If you are unsure about your typing ability, you can assess your speeds with a variety of online typing tests (simply type 'online typing tests' into your search engine – or see **typeonline.co.uk**). The Police Communications Officer's role requires a minimum typing speed of around 30/35 words per minute and ideally your speed should be higher. If you find that your speed is borderline, you have two options:

- Attempt to increase your speeds through practicing typing passages on the various websites to improve your speeds or from passages of your choosing.
- If you have been invited to an Assessment Centre and your time to improve your speeds is limited, you

may wish to download formal typing tutorials available online. Most of the websites offer the option of a free trial or free basic lessons. In addition, we have provided links to audio and typing tests in Chapter 5 that will test your ability to listen to a 999 call and accurately record information, which we trust you will find useful.

- 'Typing races' are also available online to help you to improve your speed and have fun in the process!

Additional Skills

We have included a section in Chapter 5 on how to improve your numeracy and literacy skills in preparation for attendance at the Assessment Centre.

IS THE POLICE COMMUNICATIONS OFFICER POSITION RIGHT FOR YOU?

We've already considered this previously but as we take you through the application process you may wish to repeat those questions and see if your response changes.

Only you can answer this question honestly. Our advice, as you work through this process, is to be brutally honest with yourself. It will save you from a significant amount of potential heartache later on.

CHAPTER THREE

THE APPLICATION AND SELECTION PROCESS

WHERE ARE VACANCIES ADVERTISED?

All individual police forces advertise vacancies on their websites, so it is recommended that you visit the most appropriate one for you. If there are no current vacancies, most police forces provide contact details for their recruitment section or an e-mail address where you can enquire about future vacancies. Most careers sections on police force websites are updated on a weekly basis.

Positions are also often advertised on websites like Monster (www.monster.co.uk) or Totaljobs (www.totaljobs.com) so it is a matter of continually scrutinising the job boards and police websites.

You can also create an alert on aggregator job sites like Indeed (www.indeed.co.uk) which will e-mail regular updates for the jobs that you specify.

OUTLINE OF THE SELECTION PROCESS

The recruitment procedure for the position of Police Communications Officer is straightforward. Once you have located a suitable vacancy that is still accepting applications, the fundamental steps in the process are as follows:

- Download an application form or ask for one to be sent to you in the post.
- Completion and submission of the application form. Please refer to Chapter 4 for detailed advice and guidance on completing the application form.
- If you successfully pass the initial screening of your application form, you will be invited to attend an Assessment Centre and interview which normally takes place over half a day, possibly more. Full details of what to expect at the Assessment Centre are available in Chapter 5. Preparing for the interview is covered in Chapter 6.
- You will be informed of the outcome of your application shortly after your attendance at the Assessment Centre and interview.
- A job offer is normally subject to receipt of satisfactory references and requires you to pass a pre-employment medical screening.

ON THE JOB TRAINING

All Communications Officers attend over five weeks of training to equip them with the necessary skills to carry out the requirements of the job successfully. After that a further five weeks of one-to-one coaching is provided. All candidates must successfully pass this training to continue in employment.

This will be in addition to the stringent Assessment Centre tests that you must attend and pass to progress beyond your application, coupled with extensive background checks.

If you pass all of the required tests, you will also need to develop additional skills that will enable you to carry out the responsibilities of the role successfully.

The training will be rigorous and intense, including the following:

- You will understand how to recognise and assess the severity of a 999 call and evaluate the type of response needed.
- You will learn to manage the responses of the person on the other end of the call until help arrives in many cases.
- You will learn how to communicate clearly and react quickly in a crisis (most of us start to speak rapidly and sometimes unintelligibly when faced with an imminent crisis. This cannot happen in a Communications Officer's position).
- You will be trained in how to use all necessary equipment, including a headset, radio, telephone and dispatch systems.

- You will learn how to take calls and reroute them as required.

This list is not exhaustive but gives you an indication of what is required in the role.

You will also need to be able to differentiate between real and prank calls and handle calls which are irrelevant. To put this into perspective, at the end of 2011, Manchester's police force released details of unnecessary 999 calls from the public in an attempt to reduce the number of prank calls they received. These incredibly included a man enquiring about why his turkey wouldn't defrost and a woman complaining that thieves had stolen her snowman!

ELIGIBILITY FOR EMPLOYMENT AS A POLICE COMMUNICATIONS OFFICER – VETTING

There are basic criteria you must meet in order to be considered eligible to apply for a position within the police force, regardless of what position it is. Generally, most police forces adopt the same criteria which include:

Minimum Age

You must be at least sixteen years old to apply for a position within the police force; sometimes a minimum age of eighteen may be specified. In applying, you must be able to clearly demonstrate your competence for the basic essential skills we have previously detailed.

Minimum Qualifications

Each position within the police force requires different qualifications but as we have indicated earlier, the role of Communications Officer generally requires a minimum of four GCSEs at Grade C or above (we would recommend five), together with basic literacy and numeracy skills. As we have mentioned several times, both your literacy and numeracy skills will be stringently tested.

Requirements for Residency and Nationality

To be eligible for a position in the police force, all applicants must be either a:

- British citizen
- Commonwealth citizen
- Citizen of the Republic of Ireland.

Alternatively, candidates from the European Community or EEA (European Economic Area) will be considered subject to certain restrictions.

Foreign national candidates or those from within the Commonwealth must generally include a photocopy of their passport within their application as proof of their freedom from restrictions. Additional evidence may be required to be produced but this will depend on individual circumstances.

For all candidates, there should be no restrictions on their employment status and they should be able to provide proof of having lived within the UK or EEA for a minimum of three years.

Applicants for the Police Communication Officer Role are normally required to have at least two and half years remaining on their visa before applying for the position due to the extensive training required. Any candidates who have been living in the UK for less than three years prior to the date of application are not accepted. The only exceptions to this situation apply to British service personnel working overseas, for example, the Army, RAF, Royal Navy and diplomatic personnel.

Both criteria for nationality and residency must be met for your application to be considered.

A NOTE ON CRIMINAL CONVICTIONS

If you have previously received a caution or conviction for an offence, this will not necessarily eliminate you from consideration for the role of Communications Officer. It will largely depend on the type of offence and when it was committed.

What will eliminate you instantly from the application process will be your failure to declare previous or current convictions or cautions. Honesty and transparency is essential from the outset.

If you are unsure as to what information to include, specific information will be provided by individual police forces. The general guidelines, however, including the following requirements of the details to include:-

- All offences and/or convictions and formal cautions received from the police. These include all of those which may have been received under the age of 18 (referred to as juvenile convictions). You must also declare any binding over orders which may have been imposed on you by the courts.
- If you have any current charges or police summons outstanding these must be declared.
- Traffic convictions, including drink driving, motoring and speeding offences must be included.
- You must declare any involvement in criminal investigations, whether or not they resulted in a prosecution.

The golden rule is that ***if in doubt, include the details within your application***. We must stress again that failure to do so will result in your application being terminated. In addition, due to the Data Protection Act the police force to which you have applied will not be able to disclose what information has resulted in you being eliminated from the recruitment process for the role.

A further vital point to note: The checks will incorporate your immediate family so you will need to advise them that enquiries are being made and include any information requested by the police force as necessary.

Medical Information

All employees within the police force are required to be in good physical and mental health appropriate to the position they have applied for. As part of this, a medical assessment will be carried out during the recruitment process. For the Police Communications Officer this will normally take place after you have been offered the position.

The assessment will normally include completion of a pre-employment questionnaire and possibly a report from your doctor or a medical examination if necessary.

Additional Information

Most police forces will also specify the following criteria for applicants for all of their jobs. All applicants will normally be subject to a CRB (Criminal Records Bureau) check and a credit check. For this reason, it is again important to declare any CCJs (County Court Judgements), previous bankruptcy or current or past IVA (Individual Voluntary Arrangement). Depending on the individual police force, this may affect your eligibility for the role of Police Communications Officer.

CHAPTER FOUR

APPLYING FOR A POLICE COMMUNICATIONS OFFICER ROLE

HOW TO APPLY FOR A POLICE COMMUNICATIONS OFFICER ROLE

As we have advised previously, vacancies for Police Communications Officers are normally found on the individual force websites. Once you have found a vacancy that is suitable for you, you can either request or download an application form and/or an information pack. Information packs are normally sent out to you within five working days.

Prior to Applying

All police forces will require you to check your ability to meet the basic criteria listed in the previous chapter where we looked at eligibility for the position. In addition, you must study the criteria for the role very closely and ensure you clearly understand the job description and that you can meet all of the required competencies. If there are any of the basic criteria which you cannot meet or several competencies that you do not possess then you may wish to reconsider applying when you can successfully meet all of the requirements.

HOW TO COMPLETE THE APPLICATION FORM

The standard procedure for the recruitment of Police Communications Officers is carried out by the completion of a specific Application Form that all candidates must complete in order to progress through the recruitment process.

While it can be frustrating for some candidates to have to complete an application form when they have spent time and care crafting an outstanding CV, there are two distinct advantages to completing the standard form:

- It allows each candidate to be assessed equally in comparison to others.
- It will help you to work closely on evaluating the parts of your background and skills that are relevant to the role which aren't necessarily apparent through a cursory glance of your CV.

Tip: *No matter how tempting, do not send your CV along with the application. First of all, it will be disregarded and secondly, it will suggest that you have not read the instructions for completing the application form.*

You may feel that it will expand on any additional information that the police assessor may require but your assumption would be incorrect. As attention to detail is a key skill required for the Police Communications Officer you may find that you have failed at the very first hurdle.

The Information Pack

Once you have received or downloaded the application form and information pack, you will normally find the following information:

- **Application Form** – Including guidance notes on how to complete the form.
- **Job Description** – This will include the responsibilities of the actual vacancy.
- **Person Specification** – As you will have seen from the previous examples, this will list the key skills and competencies required for the Communications Officer's role.
- **Equal Opportunities Monitoring Form** – This a basic form used to monitor equal opportunities

THE PURPOSE OF THE APPLICATION FORM

The application form itself will be used to assess your suitability for interview and also used as a basis for the interview itself. It is therefore essential to take your time to summarise and explain your achievements that relate specifically to the Police Communications Officer's role.

Allow yourself ample time to prepare your response; do not leave it until the last minute or a few days before. Thorough preparation and commitment will reflect in your application and increase your chances of being invited for an interview. If you are genuinely interested in the position, completion of the form should be taken very seriously.

Follow the advice in this document and hone your application to be the best it can be to reflect your strengths and suitability for this post in the best possible light.

OVERVIEW OF THE SELECTION PROCESS

Broadly speaking, the recruitment process will incorporate the following stages:

Stage 1 – Completing the Application Form – Ensure that you complete the application form within the specified closing date for the advert. Whether you are mailing your application or submitting it online, make a note of the closing date and ideally allow ample time to submit it before the due date. Even if you have completed the form weeks before don't wait until the very last day to submit your form. If you are relying on online submission and either your internet connection or the website is suffering from technical problems on the day, you'll have missed your opportunity. Equally, if you are sending your application by post, it's worth paying extra for recorded or special delivery to avoid it becoming lost or mislaid.

Stage 2 – Initial Candidate Screening – This is also referred to as an 'initial paper sift' where your details will be checked against the basic criteria required for the position which we looked at in the section on Eligibility. If you can tick all of the boxes in the categories on nationality, residency and previous convictions, your application will be processed into the next stage.

Stage 3 – Shortlisting – Again, this can be referred to as a 'job specific paper sift'. After Stage Two is completed, your completed form will be passed to the relevant department to where you are applying and stringently assessed against the specific requirements presented for the role. You will find these requirements in the vacancy advertisement and within your information pack. You will also find the details in Chapter 2 of this book. If you fail to meet the criteria, you will be advised at this point that you have been unsuccessful in your application.

Stage 4 – Interview and Assessment Centre – Assuming you successfully pass the first three stages, you will be invited to an interview and an Assessment Centre. The interview itself will be 'competency based', that is, you will be asked a set of questions which will ask you to give examples of certain skills.

In addition to the interview you will be asked to take a number of tests, for example, a typing test, together with role play, psychometric testing and possibly group exercises. The details will depend on the individual police force but you will be advised in advance of what to expect on the day. We have provided additional information on the Assessment Centre in Chapter 5. All candidates will be asked an identical set of questions to ensure equal comparison across the board. It is possible that the interview will take place during the Assessment Day.

A Note on Competency Based Interviews

A competency based interview is a systematic interview. Each question is focused on a specific competency related to the position of Communications Officer. All candidates will be asked questions relevant to their previous or current employment or their behaviour in a set of detailed circumstances. The interview is looking for specific examples in the response.

The assumption made at a competency based interview is that your past behaviour will be a key indicator of your future performance which will allow the interviewer to assess your ability for the role. Detailed advice on how to prepare for your interview is in Chapter 6.

Stage 5 – Health Declaration Form – Assuming you have managed to successfully come through all of the various stages and passed the Assessment Centre evaluation, you will be made a provisional offer of employment. This will be subject to various screening, health and reference checks. Your current employer will not necessarily be contacted at this stage. As part of this, you will be asked to complete a Health Declaration Form. If further information or tests are required as a result of your answers provided within this form you will be placed on what is referred to as 'medical hold' pending further investigation. For candidates living with a disability, appropriate adjustments will be made to take this into account.

If you are not successful following your attendance at interview or the Assessment Centre you will be informed in writing. Unfortunately, it is unlikely that you will be provided with feedback on why you were unsuccessful..

HOW TO COMPLETE THE APPLICATION FORM

Stage 1 – Completing the Application Form

Completing the application form is a lengthy and time consuming process and it is worth starting with your ultimate goal in mind; that is to secure an invitation to interview. To achieve this you must demonstrate on your application form that you are suitable for the role by providing examples of your experience. The environment they have been acquired in is largely irrelevant as long as you possess them.

Take a look through the advertisement for the vacancy, job description and person specification again and note the criteria before beginning to fill out your application form

This is your one and only opportunity to sell yourself and provide evidence that you meet each of the specific criteria.

A Point to Consider – The structure of the application form for the Police Communications Officer's role can vary from police force to police force. Some forms will merely provide a blank sheet and ask you to provide details of how you meet the key criteria for the position. Alternatively, some application forms specify each individual skill or competency and ask you to provide separate paragraphs in response to each question to show that you meet the required criteria. We have included examples of both within this book as a whole.

Information You Should Include

Within your answers you should provide as much information on your experience, knowledge and skills as you can that is relevant to the Communications Officer's role. This should preferably be given through examples of where you have done this in your current or previous positions. If you cannot do this, you can use domestic, social or educational examples provided that they are relevant to the role. In addition, they must ideally be taken from recent experiences.

One Essential Tip: *You must ensure that you read every question carefully and that you are answering that question succinctly.*

Structure of Answers

You can use bullet points or highlight different areas with separate headings, provided that it can be clearly understood by the assessor.

Tip: *If you are asked to provide one answer, ensure you keep it to one. Resist the temptation to provide more and do not exceed the space provided. The only exception to this is* *where you are advised that you can continue on a separate sheet when providing information on competencies.*

We cannot stress enough the importance of attention to detail in your application form.

Remember To Sell Yourself

The assessor who is evaluating your application form doesn't know who you are. All he or she will know about you and your ability will be based on the information and examples provided within your application. Ensure that you take the opportunity to provide every relevant detail as succinctly as possible and don't be afraid to sell yourself. Be confident in your abilities and what you can bring to the role.

If you are struggling to provide examples that emphasise your suitability for the role, highlight the experience you do have relevant to the responsibilities of the Communications Officer's role. If you are still failing to come up with suitable information, try and give examples of your willingness and adaptability to learn a whole new set of skills or possibly refresh previously used skills.

Be Specific

Don't simply describe the duties performed or inadvertently provide a job description of your current role. Similarly, you need to do more than state 'I have excellent communication skills'. All candidates can claim that they possess excellent communication skills but you need to provide clear examples of where you have demonstrated those communication skills.

Competency Based Questions

The selection process followed by the Police Force is what is called a 'competency-based' recruitment process. Competency based questions are behavioural questions used to determine whether or not you are the most suitable person for the job. When completing the application form you will be asked to refer to the job description and person specification and provide evidence of how you meet those skills and competencies for each of the required categories.

You must be systematic in completing your application form and ensure a concise and clear structure. Each point must be addressed as described on the job description and person specification.

We have included specific sample answers in the next section.

Now let's take a look in more detail at the actual application form itself. We have included a copy within the Appendix to this document.

Before You Begin Writing

Read and then read again the guidance notes and instructions on how to complete the application form, which will be included in the application pack.

Look Carefully Again at the Job Description and Person Specification

As we will show in our sample answers, you should be able to understand exactly what skills, experiences and competencies are required for the role of Police Communications Officer.

Think about the questions on the application form and how you are going to provide clear and concise evidence of your skills, experience and knowledge for the role.

Think Carefully About Your Knowledge and Experience

Can you show how your previous experience is relevant to the post? By carefully evaluating your career to date, you will notice a number of transferable skills used in your everyday life. Don't dismiss experience you may have gained through involvement in voluntary work or within the wider community.

If you have specific examples of responsibilities that match the requirements of the Communications Officer's role during the course of your career be sure to include them. As we mentioned above, if you are struggling to provide suitable examples, think about relevant situations in your non-professional life. These must be both relevant and recent to be effective.

Make Sure You Read the Application Form

Make sure you read the application form carefully and start to think about the answers to questions and how you are going to structure your application form. Consider using bullet points as this breaks down the text and can be clearer to read. Whatever you use, make sure you feel confident and comfortable with it. It is the content that is the most important issue coupled with your ability to answer the questions that is important.

Why Are You Interested In The Job?

Will it broaden your skills or enhance your experience? Will it represent a promotion or a good career move? Do you have other reasons for applying? Will it enable you to fulfil your aspirations and 'give something back?'

If you are currently employed, the following information might help you in answering the question above. It lists the five fundamental motivators that most people give as reasons to change jobs.

- **Culture** – The culture of the current role doesn't match your core values or long-term aspirations. Why does the Communications Officer's role appeal to you?

- **Career** – Are the long term prospects more attractive than your current role?
- **Salary** – Most job seekers look for a position that is at least equal to their current position with regard to salary and preferably better. It is the long-term prospects that often make the difference if the salary is the same.
- **Company** – You admire the culture of the company you are going to – in this case a public sector role where you will be making a clearly defined contribution to public life.
- **Leadership** – The leadership must be respected and clearly defined, which it certainly is within the police force as a whole.

It is useful at this stage to take some time to reflect on why you are applying for the role again. We have considered a number of questions earlier in Chapter 2. Read them again and consider the five basic motivators above.

What is most important to you?

Now you can begin to draft out your responses

Write Out A Draft

By drafting out your application form, it will help you to avoid mistakes on the final version, enabling you to review it and present your information in a clear and concise way. It will also allow you the opportunity to review it at your leisure. Don't forget to pay careful attention to your spelling and grammar. We will be reminding you of this on a regular basis!

Career History

When listing your career history ensure that dates are correct and in order, starting with the most recent first.

You may find the following tips useful:

- Use your previous experience relevant to the post and relevant skills and competencies
- Gear your application to the role of Police Communications Officer.
- Write in a concise, well organised and positive way. Remember to refer to your best and most recent examples in a previous role. If you can't do this then think of instances from other aspects of your life, from your time at college or from personal experiences.

GUIDELINES ON COMPLETING THE APPLICATION FORM – SECTION BY SECTION COMMENTARY

In the Appendix to this book we have included a sample Application Form. Below you will find a section by section commentary to assist you while you are filling out the various sections.

Instructions for Application

This section will provide basic advice, such as, not to include your CV with your application and how to complete the boxes. If you are advised to complete the sections accurately and honestly, ensure you do just that and note any instructions to write in 'N/A' (not applicable) where appropriate.

General

This will be your basic details, such as your name, contact details, e-mail and National Insurance Number. Be sure to provide all of your personal contact details and personal e-mail address, rather than a work based address to ensure confidentiality if you are already employed.

Driving Licence

Only complete this if it is clearly stated in the job description or person specification. Not every Police Communications Officer application will require this information.

Declaration

Don't forget to read, sign and date the application. If you are applying via e-mail, forward a scanned copy of your signature if possible. Electronic signatures are generally acceptable, however.

Qualifications

List all of your qualifications, starting with the highest level of education and working backwards. Whatever qualifications you have, you must take the necessary documentation to interview with you. You may be required to include copies within your application.

For example, begin with a degree or post graduate qualification if you have one, then any relevant 'A' Levels and GCSEs. Recognised diplomas and NVQs should also be included.

Training

Include any work based – or personally taken – training courses, that may be relevant to the position of Police Communications Officer. You may have taken specific training courses to increase your typing speed for example. You may also be trained in customer care or customer service techniques. In addition, you may have taken an Advanced Driving Test which, while not necessarily relevant for this role, would be useful within the police force in the longer term.

Membership of Professional Bodies

It doesn't matter what your background is, if you have a

professional membership of a recognised industry body it is worth including it as an indication of the level of your professionalism. For example, an HR Professional may have a membership of the Chartered Institute of Personnel and Development. While it may not seem relevant on paper, an ability to handle and manage people in stressful situations is a clear requirement of the Police Communications Officer's role and HR Professionals often have to deal with personal crises in the life of employees. The skills are transferable and relevant so think carefully about your background and qualifications and include anything you deem necessary.

Employment History

Adhere clearly to the instructions here and provide only the information asked. Normally it will be basic information; that is the name of the employer who you worked for, the dates you were employed, the position you held and your reason for leaving. There may be space for basic duties but it will be limited space so write 'customer service management, 'managing team priorities' and so on. Be concise – you probably won't have much room to be anything else.

Three points you should also note in completing this part of the application form:

- Provide your career history in reverse chronological order unless specified otherwise; simply put, begin with your current role or most recent position.
- Always be honest when providing your reason for leaving previous positions. The truth will come out during your interview or reference checks.
- Explain any career gaps. You will be asked about them at interview so always provide honest answers. It is not unusual for candidates to take a gap year, or

take time out to bring up young children. If you were unemployed at any point in your career and carried out voluntary work, include that in your career history. It demonstrates initiative and self-motivation – both key competencies required for the role of Police Communications Officer.

Referees

Think carefully about who you wish to ask to provide references regarding your suitability for this role. Some police forces may stipulate that they require a reference from the relevant HR Department in which case you will have to comply. Failing that, think of line managers or colleagues you have worked with who will focus on your strengths and suitability for the role.

Your current employer will not be contacted unless you are successful at the actual interview and assessment stage so you can be assured of confidentiality. You may have the option to state that you do not wish your current employer to be contacted without your prior permission. It will not damage your chances if you decide to check that box at this stage but your employer will be contacted for a reference if you are successful.

If you have concerns about what your employer may say regarding your abilities, remember that it is illegal for an employer to provide a negative reference. For this reason many only confirm dates of employment and the specific job an employee carried out as a standard recruitment procedure.

Skills and Competencies

Each police force will vary as to how you should complete the information on skills and competencies. Here we have taken the key skills and criteria from the person specification provided in Chapter 2 and provided sample responses to each specific requirement. This is a suggestion only of how to respond and you should make your response personal to you and reflect your personality and approach.

You will also have the option to continue on a separate sheet within this section and it is likely that you will need to do so. This is the exception to the rule of using the space provided within the application form. While it is important to be concise and summarise, you also need to clearly demonstrate your ability to meet the criteria for the position in order to be approved for interview and invited to attend the ASSESSMENT Centre.

Pause for Thought: If you are still struggling to extract examples relevant to the key competencies from the content of your CV then as we have stated earlier it may be that at this time in your career the Police Communications Officer's role is not right for you.

In this case and if it is a type of role that really interests you, don't be disheartened.

Set yourself a goal to identify the areas in which you require more experience or training and try and ascertain whether you can do this in your current situation. Additional training will require a commitment of both time and possibly money if you are not able to adapt or learn new skills within your current environment.

SAMPLE RESPONSES TO PERSON SPECIFICATION CRITERIA

Criteria: Demonstrate outstanding communication skills, both written and verbal. Candidates must possess the ability to quickly establish both the customer needs and the nature of the policing response required.

Response: My current role as a customer services call handler requires me to answer incoming calls from customers who have received faulty or incorrect products in response to orders they placed. As part of my role, I must remain calm and listen carefully to their complaints, while also being assertive if I feel they are particularly unhappy with the situation. I must also observe customer policy and focus on providing a positive experience for the customer. I had to speak to my line manager yesterday about a customer who had been waiting 2 weeks for a product. By communicating well with the customer I was able to deliver excellent customer service and offered my sincere apologies for the poor service received. He received the product the next day, together with some vouchers to spend in a well known retail store and a 10% discount on his next order.

Criteria: Demonstrate an excellent ability to listen and subsequently interpret information before conducting an accurate risk assessment based on the information provided.

Response: I was asked to deal with a particularly distressed customer who felt that the product she had received wasn't as described when she made her order. By listening to her concerns and how she described making the original order, I realised that she had made a mistake during the ordering process and clicked onto the wrong product. I explained what I thought she had done, advised her not to worry, as I understand the website can be misleading if you are not used to it and rectified the situation. This prevented a customer complaint – against which my department is assessed – and the customer was very happy with the result. She eventually wrote a letter of thanks for my patience and ability to resolve the situation.

Criteria: Show resilience in pressured situations, especially when dealing with stressful situations and often extremely emotional customers

Response: I had an experience of this situation earlier this month in my position within the Customer Feedback Department. One customer had ordered a gift for his terminally ill wife which arrived three weeks later than we had originally indicated. Unfortunately, during that time she passed away. The customer was extremely distressed by both the late delivery and also the fact that we had contacted his late wife for customer service feedback. I apologised sincerely and arranged for the company to collect the gift from the customer and also to refund the money to his account with an additional £10 as a gesture of apology. As the funeral was still to take place, the company sent a note of condolence and a wreath to the service. The customer later rang and thanked me for my understanding at a difficult time.

Criteria: Ability to make decisions quickly and appropriately based on the information provided.

Response: This actually happened while I worked in the design department of my previous employer. I was required to proof read a client's brochure after it had gone to print and found a typing error in the content. I had to make a quick decision on what to do as this was our most important client. My manager was on holiday so I was the only person available to make a decision. I cancelled the print run before it was completed pending the corrections. It did cost the department money it had not budgeted for but less than it would have done for the whole of the print run. My supervisor was relieved that I used my initiative and the client was very happy with the overall product.

Criteria: Demonstrate an ability to work effectively within a team and a willingness to support their colleagues in achieving their goals.

Response: I currently work as a business analyst carrying out telephone surveys with my clients. Last month we were asked to provide a proposal for a project with a new client. The person normally responsible for it was overseas on business so I agreed to help, working overtime for two weeks to ensure we obtained all the relevant information to be successful in the proposal. We were ultimately awarded the contract and I received a small bonus for helping out.

Criteria: Show an adaptability to both learn and retain relevant information.

Response: In my role as Telesales Manager, I was recently given a whole new set of products to sell to customers while carrying out my follow up calls. This required constant references to the new information while making customer enquiries. I was able to quickly memorise the key selling points of the products and sold five of them during my first morning sales session.

Criteria: Display an appropriate level of assertiveness when necessary.

Response: In my role as Customer Complaints Officer I am regularly required to display a degree of assertiveness when customers are 'trying it on'. One customer claimed that she had ordered a product which she had not received, although the money had been taken from her account. This wasn't the first time we had experienced this issue with this particular customer. Fortunately, we were in possession of a signed receipt from the Post Office to say the parcel had been delivered. Her husband was the signatory on this occasion. I was able to provide her with this evidence and she withdrew the complaint after her initial hostility. The situation did not recur.

Criteria: Display skills in basic research and extracting information when relevant to customer needs.

Response: Again, in my role as Customer Complaints Officer I was selling the new products that I was still unfamiliar with to my customers. One asked specific questions about the context of the products and where they were used. This was regarding the function of our kitchen ware at a specific temperature. I was able to quickly extract the information by researching our new website mock-up and provide her with what she needed to know. She was really pleased and ordered two dozen items for her new industrial kitchen.

Criteria: Show a clear focus on and understanding of community needs.

Response: This answer is drawn from experience in my personal life. Our community has been struggling since the threatened closure of a playgroup during school holidays due to budget cuts. My father is a council member and I was able to persuade him to let me arrange a meeting to discuss how we could arrange voluntary supervision of the playgroup among the local parents. During the meeting, the council partly fund the project on the condition that we would raise the shortfall within the community. My understanding of community needs was a clear benefit to the community in this situation.

Criteria: Demonstrate a clearly high level of self-motivation and an ability to work with minimal supervision. This should be evidenced through high levels of productivity.

Response: While working as a Telesales Assistant when I first joined my current employer, my line manager was suddenly off ill and I was left to set my own sales targets (with agreement) broken down into key performance indicators, that is, number of calls made, number of customers spoken to, positive responses, leads and actual orders. Within the two weeks my manager was off sick I managed to exceed all of the key performance indicators and bring in three brand new customers. I received a quarterly bonus on top of our team bonus for my efforts.

Criteria: Demonstrate a positive and flexible attitude and an ability to adapt to changing situations and new working practices.

Response: Last year, our company was bought out by a venture capitalist group to save us from going into administration. My role had some extra responsibilities added to it involving quality assurance which I was not familiar with. With some training I began to understand the requirements and adapted the audit side of the work into each of my customer orders. This was a fluid and constantly changing situation for several weeks with a high degree of uncertainty but I made every effort to ensure both the customers and the new owners were satisfied.

From the above examples, you can see that there is a framework for you to structure your answers to match the competency based criteria. Think of a recent example relevant to the above questions in your own career and following the structure below in your answer:

Describe the context – Working as a customer services operator answering incoming calls from customers who had not received the correct order.

Explain the actions you took that demonstrate your competency – Listened carefully to the customer, remained calm but assertive and escalated problem to superior.

Conclude with your result – Having escalated the issue to your line manager you were able to arrange delivery of the goods within 24 hours.

If that sounds daunting, a useful method of preparing your answers is using the STAR system. It is very similar to that provided above but some applicants find it is easier to remember the information required in the answer:

S – Situation. This is the specific context to provide you with the information. Try and be as detailed as you can without using the names of people or client companies.

T – Task. This is the actual detail of the issue you were facing and who you had to work with to achieve the outcome of the problem or issue.

A – Action. The action is what it suggests; what you actually did to resolve the situation you were facing. Provide as much information as you can about your personal behaviour within this context. Always focus on the use of 'I', rather than 'We'; unless you are being asked to provide examples of working within a team.

R – Results. What was the outcome of your action and how did it affect those around you, whether they were customers or colleagues?

You may also find the following additional tips useful in preparing your STAR-based responses:

- Ensure that your examples match those required for the role of Police Communications Officer. The advantage of the police force is that they clearly define the competencies. In many jobs you have to work them out for yourself.
- Be concise in your answer, you will only have a limited space.
- Avoid criticism of colleagues or employers in your responses, inadvertently or otherwise. It reflects badly on you and suggests a level of immaturity. The role of Police Communications Officer requires a high level of emotional maturity.

Use your best and most recent examples to make sure your responses are current. Your examples need to be of an appropriate nature. They should be specific and relate to what you did as an individual, not the team or group. Don't waffle or state irrelevant details or make assumptions that the person assessing your application will understand local practices or procedures.

Your answer does not necessarily have to be perfect or result in a positive outcome. The important factor is that you can demonstrate your experience of dealing with a particular scenario or situation and that where necessary you have learned from the experience and applied those lessons in future situations.

Supplementary Information

Here you will be required to provide any information about previous convictions, cautions or offences. You will also be asked to provide information on any personal involvement in a criminal investigation or persecution, whether or not it led to a charge against you. The key here, as we have recommended before, is to be completely honest. Failure to disclose all relevant information which may be revealed during a routine check will mean you are ejected from the recruitment process without explanation.

Membership of Organisations

You must declare your membership, either current or expired, of specific organisations. These will normally include The National Front or the British National Party as will be considered during the application process and may affect your eligibility to proceed.

Work Permit

If applicable, you will be required to provide information on your eligibility to work in the UK and whether or not you require a Work Permit. If you do, you must be able to provide proof of this permit, together with the length of time remaining on it.

Disability

If you do have a recognised disability, you will be asked whether or not you wish to declare this within your application form. This is a personal decision and you are not legally obliged to do so. As long as you meet the minimum requirements for the Police Communications Officer's role, this will not be detrimental to your job application. This will only affect you if you need any adjustments to be taken into consideration for your interview.

Equal Opportunities Monitoring

Finally, you will be asked to complete an Equal Opportunities Form covering areas like your ethnic origin and your sexual orientation. This is to ensure that all police forces adequately represent the wider community through adopting a recruitment strategy that favours diversity.

In addition, you may be required to answer questions on the following areas:

Availability for Interview

You will normally be asked to provide any dates that you cannot attend an interview or Assessment Centre. Remember that you will probably need a day off work for your participation at the latter.

Job Share

Some Police Communications Officer roles may be available on a job share basis with some police forces. If this is of interest to you, you will be given the opportunity to state it within the application form.

Former Involvement with Police or Military

You may be asked to provide details of previous employment within the police force, even on a voluntary basis and any military background, that is, employment with the Armed Forces.

Additional Vetting

Some application forms will require a separate section for vetting, including:

Family Members

This will include your spouse or partner – whether or not you are cohabiting – and family members. This will also include any former spouses or partners from whom you have separated or divorced in the previous three years and any who have died during that time.

You will also be required to list close family members over the age of 10 years including parents, step-parents, half brothers and sisters and other adults living with them.

Please note: *It will be assumed that you have advised all people named within the form that they will be vetted during your application process.*

Financial History

You may be asked questions about IVAs, CCJs, repossessions or bankruptcy affecting either you or your partner or spouse, together with details of dates. It is essential that you disclose these. This may mean that you are excluded from being considered for the Police Communications Officer role depending on the policy of the individual police force. It may be tempting to omit them and hope for the best in that case but we would recommend that you don't. They will be revealed in any background check and you will be eliminated from the process if you have not disclosed them in your application.

Not all forces automatically eliminate your application, particularly if you meet the remaining criteria and any issues that you experienced took place several years ago. Honest truly is the best policy.

On Completion

Once your application form is complete, send it with any additional material, such as photocopies of passports and so on and to the e-mail address or postal address indicated on the form. **May sure you take a copy of your completed application form.**

Please keep in mind that the recruitment process for the Communications Officer, as with most positions within the police force, can be quite lengthy so you may not receive a response to your application for a few weeks. Please also remember that throughout the process, everything will be confirmed in writing to you, either by post or e-mail, so you will be kept fully informed of what is happening.

TEN TOP TIPS AND ONE USEFUL ACRONYM FOR COMPLETING THE APPLICATION FORM

- Always write – or type out – a rough draft first using either a photocopy or scanned copy of the application form.
- Check that your handwriting or your typed information is legible.
- Avoid jargon wherever you can; keep your language simple and straightforward.
- Read all of the questions carefully – have you actually answered what you are being asked? Read and reread the question. What is it actually asking and have you answered it adequately?
- Read through your CV. Highlight the achievements and positions that demonstrate that you possess transferable skills that are relevant to the role of Police Communications Officer.
- Run your draft application through an online spellchecker to ensure that there are no obvious mistakes. When we've been reading and rereading a piece of writing for what seems like hours we miss the obvious typographical errors. Once you've done that, or if you've handwritten your draft, ask a trusted friend or colleague to read through it for you – preferably one or two trusted friends or colleagues if you can. Ask them to provide you with honest and constructive feedback.

- Review all of your answers. Have you explained what you did, how you did it and what the actual outcome was – that is – did it make a difference to your company?
- Keep a copy of your own for future reference so you know what you've actually said when it comes to the interview itself.
- Don't provide unnecessary information, you only have a limited space for your answers in most cases. You can safely assume that the person assessing your application will possess a thorough understanding of local procedures.
- Take your time in completing the form. Vacancies for the position of Police Communications Officer are not advertised every week; they only arise infrequently and are often oversubscribed with numbers of applicants. Make every effort to maximise your chances.

A useful acronym to remember while completing your application form is ASPIRE:

- **A – Appropriate** – All of your examples should be appropriate to the Communications Officer Role.
- **S – Specific** – Avoid generalisations, make your examples specific.
- **P – Positive** – Don't use examples that may raise doubts over your ability to meet the criteria for the job. Focus on your strengths.
- **I – Individual** – Emphasise your achievements, not those that were accomplished by a team that you were a part of.

- **R – Relevant** – Are you answering the question that is actually being asked?
- **E – Emphasise** – Provide clear explanations of the actions you took and why.

Once you have completed the application form, read through it again, bearing in mind the above points. Can you give a resounding positive answer to all of them? If you can't you will need to review what you have written and focus on the weaker areas you have identified.

CHAPTER FIVE

THE ASSESSMENT CENTRE

An Assessment Centre is a frequently used recruitment technique which will assess your suitability for a Police Communications Officer's role through a variety of different exercises.

Assessment Centres are frequently used by public sector employers and often in graduate recruitment or for roles that require a high level of team work and interaction with others.

The Police Communications Officer's role falls into all three of these categories.

For those of you who have not attended an Assessment Centre before, the following information will enable you to understand what will be expected of you on the day. If you have attended Assessment Centres for previous vacancies during your career, please do not disregard this vital section or become complacent.

Each position is handled in a different way, so the types of exercises, role play and psychometric tests will be specifically aligned with the competencies required for the job of Police Communications Officer. They may be very different to your previous experiences at an Assessment Centre.

WHAT IS THE PURPOSE OF THE ASSESSMENT CENTRE?

The Assessment Centre will allow the Police Force to gain a more in-depth understanding of the interpersonal skills of applicants. Put simply, that means how you operate within a team environment. More importantly for the Police Communications Officer role, it will assess how you perform in an extremely pressured environment.

How we perform at the Assessment Centre will allow our potential future employer to assess our culture fit for the position.

Statistics suggest that they are the most dependable method of evaluating a candidate's suitability for a position as they are assessed on their response to a number of different group situations. Some surveys indicate that they provide the employer with a 60% accuracy rate of candidate suitability compared to a rate of around 15% for recruitment via interviewing alone. This is due to the following reasons:

- The specific exercises carried out are selected to give candidates the opportunity to demonstrate as broad a range of skills and competencies relevant to the role of Police Communications Officer as possible.
- They are generally viewed as a fair reflection of candidate ability and the most in-depth way of assessing applicants based on merit, rather than qualifications and years of experience.

- Exercises carried out at Assessment Centres are based on practice rather than theory and for that reason are often seen as more effective than interviews. It is easy for candidates to express in theory how they would respond to specific situations in competency based interviews if they are well prepared. Assessment Centres will actually gauge your behaviour by putting you through various tests that assess your reactions in specifically designed situations.
- They offer candidates the opportunity to demonstrate how they will perform if selected for the role of Police Communications Officer, not simply their ability to perform well on the day in an interview.

TESTING AT THE ASSESSMENT CENTRE

Police recruitment tests carried out at Assessment Centres are often referred to as PIRT – Police Initial Recruitment Tests – or sometimes as PIR. Assessment Centres incorporate a number of tests and will vary depending on each police force.

Each Assessment Centre should, however, include the following:

- Informal time to give you the opportunity to introduce yourself to other candidates being tested on the day. You may have the opportunity to meet with other members of the police force but this may not be the case. Public sector and police force assessments vary significantly from those run by private companies and are often much more formal.
- Briefing sessions – You should be given an introduction to inform you what the day is about, together with the opportunity to ask any relevant questions.

- A series of tests which we have provided more information on below. These tests are intended to assess you against a variety of competencies, all of which are relevant for the position of Police Communications Officer. Candidates will normally be divided into groups and rotated around the various tests.

Assessments for the Police Communication Officer's role will vary with each police force but will usually take up to half a day and comprise a number of different tests. These may include group exercises, role play, numeracy and literacy tests through to the interview itself.

We have detailed the most common tests and the skills they assess below:

- Literacy Tests – to test basic grammar and word interpretation etc.
- Numeracy Tests – this will include some mental arithmetic
- Typing Tests – which will assess both speed and accuracy
- Software tests – to assess your ability with Windows based applications.
- Geography Tests – to assess your knowledge of the local area that you will be dealing with.
- Recorded Calls – which will test your ability to quickly extract information ranging from addresses, names of callers, etc. These will assess your listening ability coupled with your attention to detail and typing speeds.
- Group Exercises – assessing how you respond to working within a team.

- Role Play – there may be more than one assessment of role play. This will probably take the form of a caller reporting a crime such as a witnessing of a burglary or mugging. Here you will be required to note the critical information, such as, the number of offenders, their description, what car they were driving and the time of the offence. The role play aspect is particularly important as you will also need to demonstrate your ability to gain control of a distressed caller.
- Another type of role play may be a completely different situation. We have provided an actual sample of role play used in a Police Communications Officer's Assessment Centre below.

It is useful to bear in mind that during your assessment you will be required to demonstrate an awareness and understanding of religious and cultural beliefs, together with an awareness of disability, diversity and equality.

HOW TO PREPARE FOR THE ASSESSMENT CENTRE

When attending any interview you will need to prepare thoroughly and an Assessment Day is no different.

With the Police Communications Officer's role we recommend reviewing your application form and assessing your own strengths and weaknesses against the requirements for the role. We also recommend the following as part of your preparation for the day:

- You may or may not have the opportunity to ask questions on the day. Be prepared and have a list of questions you may want to ask which are relevant to the role or the assessment.

- Ensure you know exactly where the Assessment Centre's location is. Plan your route and if you are unsure, try a couple of practice runs. Don't be caught out on the day. The last thing you need is to arrive in a distressed state for a role that requires a clear ability to think and handle stressful situations!
- Allow yourself plenty of time to arrive early on the day, especially if you have an early morning appointment.
- Practice! Sample tests can be found online through various police websites.

When you arrive:

- It is quite possible that every social interaction you make will be observed from the moment you arrive at the Assessment Centre. Keep this in mind when interacting with other candidates and remain professional at all times.

IF YOU ARE TAKING LITERACY AND NUMERACY TESTS

Our grey matter can often take a while to respond, especially when we haven't used it properly for a while. The good news is that you can prepare for numeracy and literacy tests fairly easily through improving your ability to recognise word patterns and number patterns.

You may wish to try some of the following prior to the Assessment Centre day:

- Attempt a few word or number puzzles such as Sudoku. It is ideal for those wanting to improve their ability to rapidly identify patterns in numbers.
- If you ever needed a reason to spend a lazy weekend

morning with the cryptic crossword then here is your opportunity. Similarly, games like Trivial Pursuit and Hangman will also help you in improving your mental agility.

- Mental arithmetic is often difficult for those of us who habitually use calculators. One easy way of making a start on improving your mental agility with numbers is to add up the cost of the items in your trolley the next time you visit your local supermarket.
- Go back to basics. When it comes to Maths, the numerical tests carried out for the Police Communications Officer's role will be no higher than basic GCSE standard but if you haven't studied for a while consider revising some of those basics. You may find that practicing mental Maths and carrying out a selection of exercises in a literacy workbook will help you to clear out those mental cobwebs.
- Check your spelling and your grammar to ensure it's up to scratch. You'll find numerous websites that will provide you with details of words that are often spelt wrongly. Misplaced apostrophes are another issue; learn to differentiate between the correct use of 'it's' and 'its' if you can't already.
- As you read newspapers and magazines in the week prior to the Assessment Centre, try and avoid simply scanning through and picking out the parts you want to read. Consider the meaning of words as you read through the articles. Literacy tests are again fairly basic but the more prepared you are, the less anxious you will be on the Assessment Day.

A NOTE ON ROLE PLAY

Role play exercises are daunting experiences, particularly when carried out under close observation. They may be used in group exercise situations but more often than not are also carried out with an observer present who will assess your response to the scenario.

The role play exercises will often depict a real life situation. While you will be given comprehensive information on the role you will play, you will not have much time to prepare and it may often be a case of walking through a door into a room and being presented with your 'character'.

Communication Officer tests

Communication Officers have to deal with a wide range of callers, some of whom may be frightened, angry and distressed. If your application is successful, you'll be asked to attend one of our assessment day tests where we will assess your ability to handle these types of calls and obtain the information our police officers need.

The test that forms part of the assessment day is broken up into two parts as follows:

Test 1: Audio typing

For this test you will listen to a recorded 999 call and type up as much of the information you hear as possible. To pass the live test you will need to achieve an average typing speed of around 30 words per minute. You don't need to type word for word but you must cover all the relevant and important information and everything you type must make sense – this includes correct use of spelling and grammar.

Test 2: Call handling role play

The next test on your assessment day is a role-play to determine how well you deal with a live-call situation. You will field calls from assessment centre staff and be marked on how well you manage the call. This will include:

- Calming the caller if they are distressed
- Questioning the caller about the incident to obtain and record important information
- Ensuring you obtain and note the caller's name, address and phone number

These assessments are only designed to test if you have the potential to be a Communications Officer. This is a highly skilled role and, if you're successful, you'll be given all the training you need to begin this challenging and rewarding career.

You can download and try a number of sample police communications officer tests by going to the following website:

www.999CallHandlerTests.co.uk

FOUR TIPS FOR HANDLING ROLE PLAY

To reduce anxiety about role play the following tips may help:

Focus on the scenario – What would you do if you were a Store Manager trying to calm down a distressed parent, for example? How would you deal with the parent by taking rapid steps to find the lost child?

Be prepared to be 'dropped in at the deep end' – You may quite literally walk into a room and have the role thrust upon you with only a few minutes to prepare.

Be yourself – Respond as you would in any stressful situation. You will be constantly dealing with distressed members of the public in your new role so try and imagine you have actually been appointed to the job of Police Communications Officer during your role play, particularly during the telephone tests.

Try and relax – Role play can give you more of an opportunity to demonstrate your suitability for the position than other types of assessment such as competency interviews and psychometric tests. Make the most of it. Remember that every other candidate will be equally as nervous as you. Preparation is the key, the more you have prepared and the more confident you feel, the more you will be able to be yourself.

Typically, an Assessment Day will be used to assess all of the skills required for the Police Communications Officer's role in a variety of situations. These will include those we have already mentioned, but as a reminder you will be required to display strengths in the following areas:

- Team work
- Patience and ability to make decisions under pressure
- Social skills, including confidence and the ability to communicate
- Ability to work under pressure and respond to emergencies
- Relationship building
- Time management
- Listening skills
- Enthusiasm and motivation

- Flexibility and adaptability
- Customer service

At the same time, your general composure throughout the Assessment Centre Day will be closely observed.

PRACTICE TESTS

In Chapter 2 we discussed how to assess your typing speeds against the minimum requirements for the Police Communications Officer's role. As part of your preparation to increase your speeds and prepare for the Assessment Centre, we have provided links below to specific audio and typing tests relevant to the position. Practice really does 'make perfect' and we encourage you to attempt them several times during your preparation for the Assessment Centre. You can try out sample call handler tests at the following website.

www.999CallHandlerTests.co.uk

CREATING A POSITIVE IMPRESSION

Creating a positive impression throughout the Assessment Centre is essential from the moment you arrive. You may wish to keep the following points in mind:

Remain professional – You may be interacting with a variety of individuals, including other candidates. Don't be tempted to play the fool in an attempt to lighten the mood. Remember, this is a professional environment and you will be observed at all times. Maintain your composure throughout the day.

Listen – Take notes of any information you are given where possible and listen carefully to every piece of information you are provided with, no matter how insignificant it may seem, especially when it comes to role play. A vital part of the Police Communication Officer's role is the ability to listen and extract essential information.

Try and Relax – We know it isn't easy but if you can't relax to some degree, how will you handle the reality of the Police Communications Officer's role?

The Assessment Centre Is For Your Benefit – If the Police Communications Officer's role is really not right for you, you will certainly find out during the course of the Assessment Centre. These are only mock exercises, not the real thing. If you feel you are out of your comfort zone take some time to reflect after the Assessment Day. If it isn't the right role for you, be honest with yourself.

You May Surprise Yourself – Be prepared to be surprised. You may also discover skills and strengths that you never knew you had!

SEVEN TOP TIPS WHEN ATTENDING AN ASSESSMENT CENTRE

Remain calm – One of the key competencies which will be assessed under observation will be your ability to remain calm and composed under pressure.

Always introduce yourself – By introducing yourself to the rest of the group who you are placed with it will help to minimise anxiety among your colleagues. It will also demonstrate your ability to build rapport to your assessors – a vital aspect of the Police Communications Officer's role.

Address everyone by name – This will further enhance your ability to build rapport and put your colleagues at ease.

Putting people at ease is, of course, one of the key skills required in the role of Police Communications Officer.

Your colleagues are not your competitors – During an Assessment Day they may well be your co-workers at times. It may also be that several vacancies are available so the people you are 'competing' against may be your future colleagues. It is important that you demonstrate an ability to work with others as this is another vital part of the role.

Be your best – You need to be on top form. Put everything that is happening in your life out of your mind and focus. If you are not able to do this, then the position of Police Communications Officer may not be the most appropriate for you as it requires constant, clear focus.

Do not be negative – Do not, no matter how tempting it may be at times, be negative about your colleagues or employer if you are currently employed. It will speak volumes about you and it is not professional.

Preparation is the key! – A degree of anxiety is natural, especially when you are keen to secure the role – but thorough preparation will ensure that your natural anxiety is minimal and you can be as confident as possible on the day.

TIPS FOR PSYCHOMETRIC TESTS

During The Test

Psychometric tests can be quite daunting, even for the most experienced applicant and you may be asked to take a combination of Aptitude Tests and Personality Tests during your time at the Assessment Centre.

Personality Tests – The key to personality tests is to be completely honest in your responses and not attempt to second guess what answer is the best for the role. The principal thing to remember for the Police Communications Officer's role is that you must be adept at decision making. In this case, minimise any responses that indicate either no opinion or an 'average' view. You will not have the luxury of time or indifference in your decision making when you have a distressed victim of a mugging on the other end of the call

Aptitude Tests

Aptitude tests are a separate matter completely. These will assess your competencies and your ability to carry out the role of Police Communications Officer effectively and successfully. Some of the questions will relate to your numerical and logical reasoning ability, both basic competencies for the position.

Do Read the Question – Be sure you know how to actually answer the question in accordance with what has actually been asked. If it is a mathematical question, is the answer required in to decimal places, or in fractions? Is it even a question that can be answered accurately?

Is Accuracy or Speed More Important? – Your result will be based on both the number of questions and how quickly you answered them. It is not a race, however. Unlike many positions, speed coupled with accuracy is vital to the role of Communications Officer so while you cannot afford to waste time, you also cannot afford to guess at answers either. The final result will not be based purely on the number of questions that you answered correctly in a psychometric test. Your speed and accuracy will also be assessed.

Getting it Right – The time it takes you to complete your psychometric test will depend on your individual personality. There are several sample general psychometric tests available online which you may wish to practice with and gauge your strengths and weaknesses. You are unlikely to have much time to pause and check each one as it will be your ability to respond effectively under pressure which will be assessed. Perhaps it is possible to check the basics, especially in numerical or mathematical tests – for example – have you answered the questions as asked (providing the right number of decimal points and so on). Focus on your stronger points too so you can complete as much of the test as possible and don't panic if you don't complete it. Remember, it is more important to answer most questions correctly then to complete the test quickly with a high proportion of incorrect answers.

Be Aware of 'Distractors' – What is a 'distractor' you may well ask? Where you have a multiple choice question, these will be answers that closely resemble the correct question but are in fact incorrect answers. As an example, the right answer to a Maths question may be 2.75. Typical 'distractor' options for answers may include 2.7, 2.5 or even 27.5. If you prepare for your psychometric tests you may have encountered them beforehand but the vital point here is to be aware of them.

Preparation and paying attention to detail will reap rewards for all psychometric tests.

Don't Guess! – In a Police Communications Officer's role, you cannot guess. All decisions and assessments must be based on facts. It is a highly accountable role. As an alternative to guessing, if you are really baffled by some answers, work on the basis of elimination. If you are able, rule out the answers you know to be incorrect based on your knowledge of what the answer may be. If you know that they fall within a certain area or must be answered to a number of decimal places, you may be able to eliminate two or three of the potential responses. This will greatly improve your overall test results as the assessor will know that you have attempted to make an 'educated' guess.

Multiple Choice Responses – Many psychometric tests offer multiple choice responses and while all police forces vary, you will undoubtedly face at least one multiple choice test. The same rules apply as we mentioned above; avoid guessing in your answer if possible. Some psychometric tests utilise a system referred to as 'negative' assessments so all of your incorrect answers will be marked as a 'minus' number against your correct ones and deducted from your final score. Be aware of this and again make as 'calculated' a guess as you can if you really don't know the answer. Try and adopt a process of elimination again if feasible. Guessing will only suggest that you have a careless attitude to risk-taking which may well result in an unsuccessful application for the Police Communications Officer's role and failure on the Assessment Day.

Play To Your Strengths – Don't spend too long on answers or problems that you are struggling with. Instead, move on to other questions that you can respond to quickly and confidently. If there is time you can always come back to any questions you missed when you've completed the test.

Check The Back Of The Page! – It is not unknown for candidates taking psychometric tests to assume they have finished the test when in fact they have missed the questions on the very last page. Always turn over and check. It is all to do with attention to detail and thinking ahead, two more competencies required for the role of Police Communications Officer.

If Time Allows – If it is possible, it may be worth checking through your answers at the end of the test. It won't be possible in every case and if it isn't don't panic. You won't be the only candidate who is struggling to complete the test on time. Psychometric tests for these roles are designed to be difficult to complete in order to assess your responses under pressure.

Remember Preparation – The key to your successful performance at an Assessment Centre is no different to the key to your successful performance at interview. Preparation, preparation and preparation!

CHAPTER SIX

THE INTERVIEW

During the police communications officer interview you will get asked a series of questions that will assess your suitability for the post. In this section of the guide we will provide you with a number of sample interview questions and responses that will help you to prepare. It is important to note that you MUST provide EVIDENCE of where you meet the assessable competencies that form part of the job description. This can be achieved by responding to the interview questions using the STAR method.

S – Situation. This is the specific context to provide you with the information. Try and be as detailed as you can without using the names of people or client companies.

T – Task. This is the actual detail of the issue you were facing and who you had to work with to achieve the outcome of the problem or issue.

A – Action. The action is what it suggests; what you actually did to resolve the situation you were facing. Provide as much information as you can about your personal behaviour within this context. Always focus on the use of 'I', rather than 'We'; unless you are being asked to provide examples of working within a team.

R – Results. What was the outcome of your action and how did it affect those around you, whether they were customers or colleagues?

Now let's take a look at a number of sample interview questions and responses. Please note: the following interview questions are not guaranteed to be the ones you will get asked during the interview; however, they are useful guide for helping you to prepare.

SAMPLE QUESTION NUMBER 1

Tell us why you want to become a police communications officer?

Sample response

"I have worked in my current role now for a number of years. I have an excellent employer and enjoy working for them but unfortunately no longer find my job challenging. I understand that the role of a police communications officer is both demanding and rewarding and I believe I have the qualities to thrive in such an environment. I love working under pressure, working as part of a team that is diverse in nature and helping people in difficult situations. The public expectations of the police are very high and I believe I have the right qualities to help the police deliver the right service to the community by becoming a highly competent communications officer.

I have studied the qualities and competencies required for the role and believe that I have the skills to match them and deliver what they require."

Top tips:

- Don't be negative about your current or previous employer.
- Be positive, enthusiastic and upbeat in your response.
- Make reference to the qualities and competencies if possible.

SAMPLE QUESTION NUMBER 2

Why have you chosen this particular Police Force?

Sample response

"I have carried out extensive research into the Police Service and in particular this force. I have been impressed by the level of service it provides. The website provides the community with direct access to a different range of topics and the work that is being carried out through your community wardens is impressive. I have looked at the national and local crime statistics and read many different newspapers and articles. I like this Police Force because of its reputation and the people that I have spoken to who work within the force have told me that they get a great deal of job satisfaction from working here."

Top tips:

- Research the force thoroughly and make reference to particular success stories that they have achieved.
- Be positive, enthusiastic and upbeat in your response.
- Be positive about their force and don't be critical of it, even if you think it needs improving in certain areas.

SAMPLE QUESTION NUMBER 3

What does the role of a police communications officer involve?

Sample response

"Communications Officers are the first point of contact for members of the public requesting police support. It is a highly responsible job and one that requires a calm and reassuring nature.

They answer emergency 999 calls and high priority calls as efficiently as possible, obtaining and recording accurate information, assessing the level of police response required and initiating the appropriate action as quickly as possible.

Where no police action is required, they provide advice and guidance to the caller. In all cases, callers are dealt with in a calm, courteous and professional manner, and if necessary, firmly to obtain essential information."

Top tips:

- Understand the qualities and competencies and be able to recite them word for word when responding to this question.
- Try to speak to current serving police communications officers to try and find out more about the job that they do.

SAMPLE QUESTION NUMBER 4

Have you ever lost your temper?

This is a great interview question and is not easy to answer. All of us have lost our temper at some point, but you need to be careful as to how much you disclose. Part of the role of a communications officer is to remain calm under pressure and you need to demonstrate this in your response. They do not want to employ people who lose their temper when dealing with 999 calls. It is during these times that you will need to use your skills to calm people down and also have the ability to filter out hoax calls.

The question is designed to see how honest you are, and whether you are a naturally aggressive person. It is ok to lose your temper at times during your personal life, but it is not welcome as a communications officer.

Sample response

'In the whole I am a calm person and do not become aggressive or confrontational.

Whilst it is only natural to be annoyed with people from time to time, I see no point in losing my temper. It is just wasted energy. I understand that communications officers cannot lose their temper with callers as it would be highly unprofessional and deter from the reason why they are there; to extract the information required in order to dispatch the appropriate response in the fastest time possible. I appreciate that it must be frustrating at times dealing with hoax callers, but the way to resolve issues is to remain calm and be patient.'

Key areas to consider:

- Try to use 'non-confrontational' words and phrases during your response – patience, calm, understanding, etc.
- Demonstrate your understanding of the role and the importance of remaining calm and professional.

SAMPLE QUESTION NUMBER 5

How do you feel about working with people from different cultures and backgrounds?

This is quite a common interview question and one that you need to be prepared for. Respect for diversity is essential to the role of a communications officer as you will be dealing with and working with people from different cultures and backgrounds. We live in a diverse community that brings many positive aspects that we can learn from. When answering the question, you should be aiming to demonstrate that you are totally at ease when working with people from different cultures and backgrounds. You may wish to give an example of this in your response. Take a look at the following response to this question. Remember to be honest in your reply and only state the facts about your feelings towards people from different cultures. If you are not truthful in your response, you will not be doing yourself, or the police force, any favours.

Sample response

"I am totally at ease in those situations, in fact I don't even think about it. This has never been a problem for me. I have a sincere interest in people from different cultures and backgrounds and have learnt many things from them in the past. I would like to think that we can all learn something from everybody, regardless of their culture or background and this is a part of the job that I would look forward to.

There are so many different and exciting things to learn in life and this can only be achieved by meeting, respecting and understanding people from different cultures and backgrounds. Teams that are diverse in nature have a better chance of delivering a higher quality of service. If the community in which the police force serves is diverse, then so should the workforce that delivers the service."

Key areas to consider:

- Be honest when answering this type of question.
- Demonstrate that you understand diversity and the benefits this brings to society. Provide examples where appropriate.

SAMPLE QUESTION NUMBER 6

If you witnessed a member of your team being bullied or harassed at work what action would you take and why?

There is only one answer to this question and that is that you would take action to stop it, providing it was safe to do so. Bullying or harassment of any kind must not be tolerated. The second part of the question is just as important. They are asking you why you would take this particular action.

Before you prepare your answer to this question think carefully about what action you would take if somebody was being bullied or harassed. Taking action can mean a number of different things ranging from reporting the incident to your manager, through to intervention.

Whatever answer you give it is important that you are honest and tell the truth about how you would respond to such a situation. Take a look at the following sample response to this question.

Sample response

"I would stop it immediately if it was safe to do so. This type of behaviour is totally unacceptable and must not be tolerated in the workplace. The reason why I would take action is because if I didn't, then I would effectively be condoning the bullying or harassment. The type of action I would take would very much depend on the circumstances. In most cases I would intervene at the time of the incident and ask the person to stop the bullying or harassment.

If the incident were very serious, then I would report it to my line manager in the police control room so that further action could be taken. Whatever the situation was, I would definitely take steps to stop it from happening. I believe that I would also have a duty under Police Force policy to take action to stop bullying and harassment."

SAMPLE QUESTION 7

What do you understand about the term equality and fairness?

Treating everybody with respect and dignity is important in everyday life. Treat others how you would expect to be treated regardless of their age, gender, sexual orientation or cultural background.

If you are not capable of treating people with respect and dignity then the Police Force is not for you!

A question based on this subject is likely to come up during the interview and it relates to the quality of being able to work with others.

The following is a sample response to this question.

Sample response

"Equality and fairness is about treating people with dignity and respect and without discrimination. Unfair discrimination in employment is wrong. It is bad for the individuals who are denied jobs or who suffer victimisation or harassment because of prejudice. I understand that within the police force it is the responsibility of everyone to uphold the principles and policies of the organisation in relation to equality and fairness. Discrimination or unacceptable behaviour of any sort is not tolerated and nor should it be. Not only is it important to apply these principles whilst working with colleagues in the force but it also applies when serving the public."

SAMPLE QUESTION 8

Do you have any experience of working as a team member?

The ability to work effectively in a team is an extremely important aspect of the role. Not only will you be spending a great deal of time together at work, you will also depend on your colleagues during stressful incidents in the control room. Therefore it is important that you can demonstrate you have the ability to work as an effective team member.

When responding to this type of question, try to think of occasions when you have been part of a team and achieved a common goal.

Maybe you are already involved in team sports playing hockey, rugby or football? You may also find that you have experience of working as a team member through work. If you have no or very little experience of working as a team member then try to get some before you apply to the police force as a communications officer. After all, teamwork is an important aspect of the role.

Now take a look at the following sample response.

Sample response

"Yes I have many years' experience of working in a team environment.

To begin with, I have been playing hockey for my local team for the last three years. We worked really hard together improving our skills over the course of last season and we managed to win the league.

I am also very much involved in teamwork in my current job. I work as a nurse at the local hospital and in order for the ward to function correctly we must work effectively as a team. My job is to check all of the patients at the beginning of my shift and also make sure that we have enough medical supplies to last the duration. It is then my responsibility to inform the ward sister that the checks have been carried out. She will then obtain more supplies if we need them.

We have to work very closely together for many hours and we all pull together whenever the going gets tough. I enjoy working in a team environment and feel comfortable whilst working under pressure."

SAMPLE QUESTION 9

If a member of the public asked you how to call the Police during an emergency, what advice would you give them?

This question is not a common one but there have been occasions when it has been asked during the interview. If you are going to be a police communications officer then you certainly should know how to call the police in the event of an emergency.

The answer is a simple one and the following is a sample response to help you.

Sample response

"I would tell them to dial 999 using the nearest available working phone.

I'd also inform them that they can use their mobile phone to dial 999 even if they do not have any credit available.

I would tell them that they would be connected to a central call handling centre where they will be asked which service they require.

I would tell them that they must ask for the police. Once they are through to the operator they will be asked a series of important questions. I would tell them to listen carefully to the operator and answer all the questions carefully and accurately. It is important that they remain calm when making the call so that the operator can obtain all of the information.

I would tell them that the type of questions they will be asked are:

- *What the emergency is (e.g. burglary, car crash, flood, person trapped etc);*

- *Where it is (e.g. full address if known, name of road, prominent landmark);*
- *How many people are involved, if any?*
- *Any special problems/hazards that they need to know about.*

I would finally inform them that it is important to only use the 999 service when it is genuinely needed and that hoax calls should never be made."

SAMPLE QUESTION NUMBER 10

How do you think you would cope with working the police shift system?

Working unsociable hours is part and parcel of life in the police force. You need to be 100% certain that you can cope with the irregular shift patterns and that your family supports you. Take a look at the following sample response.

Sample response

"I believe I would cope very well. I have taken into consideration the fact that I would be required to work unsociable hours and I am prepared for this. I have discussed it with my family and I have their full support. I have worked office based hours for many years now and I am actually looking forward to the change."

SAMPLE QUESTION NUMBER 11

Tell me about a time when you helped someone who was distressed or in need of support?

How to structure your response:

- What was the situation?
- Why did you provide the help? (Whether you were approached or you volunteered. It is better to say you volunteered!)
- What did you do to support the individual?
- What specifically did you do or say?
- What was the result?

Strong response

Make sure you provide a specific example of where you have helped someone who was in distress or who needed your support. Try to provide an example where the outcome was a positive one as a result of your actions. If the situation was one that involved potentially dangerous surroundings (such as a car accident), did you consider the safety aspect and did you carry out a risk assessment of the scene?

Weak response

Candidates who provide a weak response will be generic in their answering. The outcome of the situation will generally not be a positive one.

Sample response

"One evening I was sat at home watching television when I heard my next door neighbours smoke alarm sounding. This is not an unusual occurrence as she is always setting off the

alarm whilst cooking. However, on this occasion, something was different as the alarm did not normally sound so late at night. I got up out of my chair and went to see if she was OK. She is a vulnerable, elderly lady and I always look out for her whenever possible. When I arrived next door I peered through the window and noticed my neighbour sat asleep on the chair in the front room. Wisps of smoke were coming from the kitchen so I knew that she was in trouble. I immediately ran back into my house and dialled 999 calmly. I asked for the Fire Service and the Ambulance Service and explained that a person was stuck inside the house with a fire burning in the kitchen. I provided the call operator as much information as possible including landmarks close to our road to make it easier for the Fire Service to find. As soon as I got off the phone I immediately went round the back of my house to climb over the fence. Mrs Watson, my neighbour, usually leaves her back door unlocked until she goes to bed. I climbed over the fence and tried the door handle. Thankfully the door opened. I entered into the kitchen and turned off the gas heat which was burning dried up soup. I then ran to the front room, woke up Mrs Watson and carried her carefully through the front door, as this was the nearest exit. I then sat Mrs Watson down on the pavement outside and placed my coat around her. It wasn't long before the Fire Service arrived and they took over from them on in. I gave them all of the details relating to the incident and informed them of my actions when in the kitchen."

SAMPLE QUESTION NUMBER 12

Tell me about a time when you had to follow clear instructions or rules in order to complete a task?

When working as a police communications officer you will have to follow clear instructions at all times. This question will assess your ability to do just that during a work situation.

How to structure your response:

- What was the work you were doing?
- What were the rules or instructions that you had to follow?
- What did you do to complete the work as directed?
- What was the result?
- How did you feel about completing the task in this way?

Strong response

The police force strives for excellence in everything it does. Therefore, it is crucial that you provide a response that demonstrates you too can deliver excellence and maintain high standards. Try to think of a situation, either at work or otherwise, where you have achieved this. Make your response specific in nature. If you have had to follow specific instructions, rules or procedures then this is a good thing to tell the panel.

Weak response

Weak responses are generic in nature and usually focus on a candidate's own views on how a task should be achieved, rather than in line with a company or organisation's policies

and procedures. The candidate will display a lack of motivation in relation to following clear instructions or rules.

Sample response

"I am currently working as a sales assistant for a well-known retailer. I recently achieved a temporary promotion and part of that role includes carrying out preopening checks. I am required to get to work 60 minutes before opening time and carry out a comprehensive routine check. The work includes checking that all fire exits are unlocked, testing the fire alarm, assessing the current stock levels to make sure we have enough for the day's trade, turning on power and heating, checking the tills are stocked with cash, carrying out a risk assessment, briefing staff on safety hazards, briefing staff on the requirements for the day and liaising with the shopping centre manager.

It is important that I follow the rules and instructions carefully because if I miss any of them off, the day's trading will not run smoothly and there could also be safety implications.

In order to make sure that I follow the instructions carefully I always make sure that I arrive at work with plenty of time to spare. This ensures that I leave plenty of time for any last minute hiccups. I also follow a self-made checklist which I carry around with me on a clip board. Once I have completed a task, I tick it off and write down any relevant notes that will help me to brief my staff. I always feel good about the manner in which I carry out my duties. I am an organised person and I take great pride in carrying out my duties both diligently and professionally."

SAMPLE QUESTION NUMBER 13

Can you provide an example of a situation when you have had to work under pressure?

The role of a police communications officer will often be required to work under extreme pressure. Therefore, the recruitment staff will want to know that you have the ability to perform in such an environment. If you already have experience of working under pressure then you are far more likely to succeed and be capable of meeting the demands of the job. When responding to a question of this nature, try to provide an actual example of where you have achieved a task whilst being under pressure. Don't forget to follow the guidance at the beginning of this section which related to responding effectively to interview questions using the STAR technique. Questions of this nature are sometimes included in the application form, so try to use a different example for the interview, if the question comes up.

Sample response

"Yes, I can. In my current job as car mechanic for a well-known company, I was presented with a difficult and pressurised situation. A member of the team had made a mistake and had fitted a number of wrong components to a car. The car in question was due to be picked up at 2pm and the customer had stated how important it was that his car was ready on time because he had an important meeting to attend. We only had two hours in which to resolve the issue and I volunteered to be the one who would carry out the work on the car. The problem was that we had 3 other customers in the workshop waiting for their cars too, so I was the only person who could be spared at that particular time. I worked solidly for the next 2 hours, making sure that I

meticulously carried out each task in line with our operating procedures. Even though I didn't finish the car until 2.10pm, I managed to achieve a very difficult task under pressurised conditions whilst following strict procedures and regulations. I understand that the role of a paramedic will require me to work under extreme pressure at times and I believe I have the experience to achieve this. I am very meticulous in my work and always ensure that I take personal responsibility to keep up-to-date with procedures and policies in my current job."

CONCLUSION

So that's it. Everything you need to know to pass the recruitment and selection process and become a Police Communications Officer (999 Call Handler).

There is no doubt that the role of Police Communications Officer meets all of the elements required for a rewarding job highlighted by the National Careers Service. While it may be appealing, however, it is by no means a job for the faint hearted!

The skills and competencies required to successfully meet the criteria for the position are both stringent and demanding. During the recruitment process you may well find yourself going beyond your comfort zone on several occasions, but this is ideal preparation for the realities of the actual role.

We hope that this guide will prove to be an invaluable part of your application and preparation process – and a vital aid to surviving the Assessment Centre and performing well at your interview.

Remember; thorough preparation coupled with an in depth analysis of your career achievements and transferable skills will equip you to perform to the best of your ability on the day.

Good luck!

APPENDIX A

POLICE COMMUNICATIONS OFFICER SAMPLE APPLICATION FORM*

* Please note that all the information contained within this application form is fictitious and to provide an example only

PERSONAL DETAILS

Notes: a) Please complete all sections accurately and honestly
b) CVS included with your application will be rejected
c) Please write 'n/a' if a section is not applicable to you

Preferred Title: (Mr/Ms/Miss/Mrs/Dr) Mr

Family Name: Doe

Forename(s): John

Home Address: 123 Private Lane
London, XX1 2PP

E-Mail Address: j.doe@fmail.com

NI Number: AA 12 34 56 78 Z

Telephone Numbers: (Including STD Codes)

Home: 0444 444 4444

Work: N/A

Mobile: 77777 444444

SECONDARY EDUCATION

From	To	School or College Name and Address	Level of Examination or Courses Passed Please Provide Grades Achieved
1996	2001	Scientific Comprehensive Science Road Warwick, W2 B24	2 'A' Levels in Information Technology, Design and Technology, both at Grade C 10 GCSEs, 7 at Grade C and above including English and Maths

FURTHER/HIGHER EDUCATION

From	To	College or University Name and Address	Level of Examination or Courses Passed Please Provide Grades Achieved
2001	2004	Warwick College Brown Road Warwick, W1 B23	BSc Honours Degree – Design and Information Technology Grade Achieved: 2:1

ADDITIONAL COURSES TAKEN FOR SPECIFIC TRAINING

From	To	Name of Provider	Course Title
2005	2008	Skilled Telephone Providers	Specialist Training in Customer Service

EMPLOYMENT HISTORY

From	To	Name and Address of Employer	Job Title and Brief Duties of the Role	State Your Reasons For Leaving
2008	Date	Computer Products Ltd Ultimate Science Park Warwick W10 8HP	Team Manager, Customer Services Manager of a team of four. Required to handle customer orders and complaints on a daily basis and deal with product enquiries.	I wish to pursue a career that will help me to fulfil my aspirations more effectively
2005	2008	Telesales R Us Communications Row Warwick W99 1ZZ	Telesales Assistant Basic telephone answering, dealing with customer enquiries and handling orders. Regularly dealing with three or four issues at once.	Career progression and to find something more relevant to my degree

RELEVANT EXPERIENCE

Please detail the skills, experience and competencies you possess that are relevant to the role of Police Communications Officer. You may wish to continue on a separate sheet

In my role as Team Manager in Customer Services I am used to multi-tasking, dealing with customer complaints and delegating urgent work within my team as necessary. My ability to quickly understand the issues facing both my team and my customers allows me to respond to any complaints or issues with customer service. I have been awarded Team Manager of the month five times in the past eight months for my handling of some difficult customer complaints, particularly with two irate customers who were pursuing legal action.

I am also adept at handling several telephone calls at once, while dealing with issues within my team. I believe that my transferable skills in this regard are ideal for the role of Police Communications Officer. I have listed on the attached sheet my response to the key competencies and examples of where my experience has been relevant.

I already have experience of working irregular shift patterns whilst working with 'Telesales R us' and I have the full support of my family with regards to this element of the role. I have worked as part of an effective team on numerous occasions and have a confident telephone manner. I also have experience with audio equipment which was obtained during my 'skilled telephone providers' course in 2008.

Finally, I believe that I have the potential to become a competent police communications officer and help the Police Force deliver a high quality service to the public.

HEALTH/DISABILITY

Do you consider yourself to have a disability? You are invited to provide this information but there is no legal requirement to do so. The definition of disability is *'the condition of being unable to perform a task or function because of a physical or mental impairment'*** which affects normal daily activities'. — No

SUPPLEMENTARY INFORMATION

Do you require a Work Permit to work in the United Kingdom, if yes, please provide photocopies of your current permit.

YES NO

PREVIOUS CONVICTIONS

Have you ever been convicted, charged, cautioned, or summonsed or bound over? Details of fixed penalty notices are also required any points incurred on your driving licence. Please also provide details of any pending prosecutions. — No

** Dictionary definition provided by www.thefreedictionary.com

REFEREES

Please give details from whom we may obtain references. One should be your present or if you are unemployed, your previous employer or college. Referees will not be approached until after interview and if you receive an offer of employment.

Current/Previous Employer	Second Referee	Third Referee
Computer Products Ltd Mr A Dickson Manager	Telesales R Us Mrs B Turner HR Director	

DECLARATION

IN ACCORDANCE WITH THE DATA PROTECTION ACT 1998, I ACKNOWLEDGE THAT THE INFORMATION PROVIDED ON THIS FORM WILL BE USED FOR THE PURPOSES OF SECTION AND INTERVIEW FOR THE ROLE OF POLICE COMMUNICATIONS OFFICER. SHOULD THE APPLICATION BE UNSUCCESSFUL, I ACKNOWLEDGE THAT THE INFORMATION PROVIDED WILL BE HELD FOR A PERIOD OF UP TO ONE YEAR.

Signed: Date:

how2become